this activity book
belongs to:

·····························

·····························

I spy with my little eye something beginning with ...

It's an

Angel

I spy with my little eye something beginning with ...

It's a

Bell

I spy with my little eye something beginning with ...

It's a

Snowman

I spy with my little eye something beginning with ...

It's a

Decoration

I spy with my little eye something beginning with ...

It's a

Candle

I spy with my little eye something beginning with ...

It's a

Bread

I spy with my little eye something beginning with ...

It's an

Elf

I spy with my little eye something beginning with ...

It's a

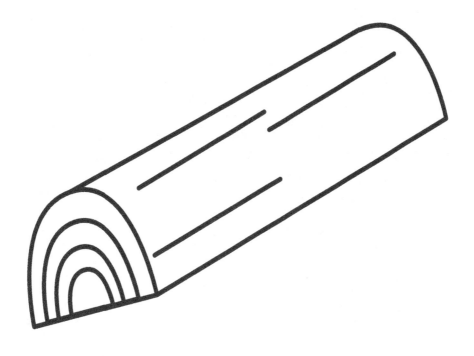

Firewood

I spy with my little eye something beginning with ...

It's a

Pie

I spy with my little eye something beginning with ...

It's a

King

I spy with my little eye something beginning with ...

It's a

Candy

I spy with my little eye something beginning with ...

I spy with my little eye something beginning with ...

It's a

Mistletoe

I spy with my little eye something beginning with ...

It's an

Ornament

I spy with my little eye something beginning with ...

It's

Santa Claus

I spy with my little eye something beginning with ...

It's an

Imp

I spy with my little eye something beginning with ...

It's a

Cake

I spy with my little eye something beginning with ...

It's a

Present

I spy with my little eye something beginning with ...

R

It's a

Reindeer

I spy with my little eye something beginning with ...

It's a

Stocking

I spy with my little eye something beginning with ...

It's

Merry Christmas

Xmas

I spy with my little eye
something beginning with ...

It's

Light

I spy with my little eye something beginning with ...

It's a

Turkey

I spy with my little eye something beginning with ...

It's a

Wreath

I spy with my little eye something beginning with ...

It's a

Gift

I spy with my little eye something beginning with ...

It's a

Sleigh

I spy with my little eye something beginning with ...

It's a

Tree

I spy with my little eye something beginning with ...

It's a

Gingerbread

I spy with my little eye something beginning with ...

It's a

Sack

I spy with my little eye something beginning with ...

It's a

Pudding

Made in United States
Orlando, FL
17 December 2024

55973111R00037